Running From The Devil

Understanding Addiction

Copyright 2023 by Jonathan Fears

All rights reserved. No part of this book may be reproduced or transmitted in any form or by any means without written permission of the author.

Running From The Devil

Understanding Addiction

By

Jonathan Fears

DEDICATION

    I dedicate this book to my awesome family. My wife Lisa, my four children (Sam, Gracie, Abigail, and Olivia), my mother, Katie, and my father, Gerald, have supported me during the hardest times of my life. When I was in active addiction, my family never left my side, and never turned their back on me. My family continues to love and support me. Without their support, I am certain this book would never have been written.
    Words can never express how much I love you!

TABLE OF CONTENTS

LESSON		PAGE
Lesson 1	"Don't Ever Give Up"	7
Lesson 2	"The Greatest of These is Love"	12
Lesson 3	"Our Guide For Hard Times"	18
Lesson 4	"We Are Our Own Worst Enemy"	24
Lesson 5	"Choose To Be Optimistic"	30
Lesson 6	"Overcoming Failure"	33

FOREWORD

      This is the first book I've ever written. All scripture references are taken from the King James Version of the Bible. Some other versions are good, but since the wording of other translations are different, you might have problems if you attempt to use other translations to fill in the blanks in this Study Guide.

      This Study Guide contains six lessons of Hope and Encouragement. Please use your Bible and answer the questions in the heart of each lesson. Discussion questions and statements are also included. If you are in a group setting, please take time to truthfully discuss these. If you're alone, give each question and statement serious thought. Wherever you may be at this moment, let this Study Guide help you move forward in forgiving yourself, and others.

      I'm a former addict. This book is created for the purpose of helping addicts and their families find peace. However, anyone can benefit from the information found within the pages of this Study Guide. Everyone can benefit from learning more about addiction. Please keep an open mind as you study this guide.

      The discussion questions and statements do not have right and wrong answers. They are designed to stimulate thought and conversation among groups and individuals.

      I have struggled with addiction at different stages throughout the course of my life. Some of my experiences are shared in this Study Guide. The Bible is used to assist in making points relevant to achieving sobriety.

      If you are in active addiction, or the family member of someone in active addiction, it's probable you have no true peace in your life at the moment. I'm sorry for this and I truly hope this Study Guide will help you find some of the peace you are looking for.

Copyright Date

the year 2023

by

Jonathan Fears

INTRODUCTION

As a former addict, I completely understand the thoughts, motives, and intentions of those struggling with addiction. I also understand the misery and emptiness felt by families who have loved ones struggling with active addiction.

Those struggling with addiction are looking to live a sober, happy, and productive life. However, there is a real problem. Those in active addiction are facing an opponent unlike any they've encountered in all their days! Satan is real and he is exactly as Jesus describes him in John 8:44, "...*he was a murderer from the beginning, and abode not in the truth, because there is no truth in him*..."

Make no mistake, Satan is behind all addictions. He works any way possible to cause us to fail. Many times, Satan presents himself to us in pill, powder, rock, and liquid forms. Few of us see what is actually happening until it's too late. Before we know it, we, or someone we care about, has made a deal with the devil. Those in active addiction feel trapped, controlled, and lost!

There are things that can be done to help those in active addiction achieve sobriety. With the help of support groups, loved ones, and God, sobriety can be obtained, and maintained. James 4:7, "*Submit yourselves therefore to God. Resist the devil, and he will flee from you.*"

When users choose to get God involved in their lives, they bring purpose to the process of recovery. It has been my experience, when we allow God to be involved in the recovery process, things are more clearly seen. I encourage my readers to simply give God a chance! I mean REALLY give Him a chance!

Feel free to contact me via email with any questions you might have. My email is fearsjon8@gmail.com. I know, and will recommend, rehabilitation facilities designed to help you or someone you care about. I am also available to give talks to groups interested in learning more truth about addiction.

I will be writing other books in the future. They will be available for purchase on Amazon.com in much the same way as this Study Guide is.

The Author

Jonathan "Jon" Fears

LESSON 1
"Don't Ever Give Up!"
2 Corinthians 12:7-9

Satan is real! He wants you to give up! He wants you to quit trying! Run! Run! Run! Keep running!

--Job 1:6, *"Now there was a day when the sons of God came to present themselves before the Lord, and _____ came also among them." (7) And the Lord said unto Satan, Whence comest thou? Then Satan answered the Lord, and said, From going to and fro in the _____, and from _____ up and down in it."*

Don't ever give up! Don't ever quit trying to make life better! Life is a funny thing! Some things make sense, some don't. One day we find it hard to get out of bed, while the next day it's much easier. It doesn't matter if the sun is shining or not. We really can't explain why. Our minds play tricks on us. We feel loved, sometimes. Other times, it seems as if nobody really cares.

It is hard for us to nail down a purpose for our life. Some of us are blessed, and have no problem ascertaining our purpose here on Earth. I am truly happy for those who can unequivocally do this, however, many of us, including this author, simply struggle from time-to-time understanding just exactly why we're here and what we're supposed to be doing. We want to know why things happen the way they do. We never seem to figure out the answer to the question, "why do things happen the way they do?" And so, we struggle.

We struggle because we have learned, through living, that life is not fair! It's not fair at all. One person may have a life free of disease while another may be sick from birth. Both were born in the same community and were raised the same way. One lives to be close to one-hundred while the other dies in their thirties. Two people may be in a traffic accident. One walks away unharmed, while the other has their life taken from them. Both were wearing seat belts. Both were doing what they were supposed to be doing. Try making sense of this.

The apostle Paul had a problem making sense of some things in his life. He states in the following verse that he has a *"thorn in the flesh"*. He never identifies exactly what it is, only that Satan was involved!

--2 Corinthians 12:7, *"And lest I should be exalted above _____ through the abundance of the revelations, there was given to me a thorn in the flesh, the _____ of _____ to buffet me, lest I should be exalted above measure."*

Paul's *"thorn in the flesh"* could have been any number of things, including bad eyesight. Evidence to support this theory can be found in Galatians 6:11 where Paul advises his readers to notice the large letter written with his own hand.

--Galatians 6:11, *"Ye see how _____ a letter I have written unto you with mine own _____."*

In addition, in Galatians chapter four, Paul praises the Galatians for their willingness to help. The following verse indicates Paul knew Christians in the region would have given him their own eyes, if possible.

--Galatians 4:15, "*Where is then the blessedness ye spake of? For I bear you record, that, if it had been _____, ye would have _____ out your own _____, and have given them to me.*"

However, we cannot say with complete confidence what Paul's "*thorn in the flesh*" actually was. Other things to consider are poor health and psychological ailments.

Paul has just finished telling his readers in 2 Corinthians 12:1-6, that God has revealed some things to him. Paul speculates his "*thorn in the flesh*" could have been given to keep him humble. He knew he mustn't forget how Jesus felt.

Paul knew he must stay humble. We, too, must stay humble. In keeping with his effort to stay humble, Paul considered himself to be the least of the apostles.

--1 Corinthians 15:9, "*For I am the _____ of the apostles, that am not meet to be called an _____, because I _____ the church of _____.*"

--Romans 12:3, "*For I say, through the grace given unto me, to every man that is among you, not to _____ of himself more highly that he ought to think; but to think _____, according as God hath dealt to every man the measure of _____.*"

Paul also knew if he allowed his "*thorn in the flesh*" to negatively affect his ministry, he would be giving Satan an upper hand.

Paul asked God three times to remove his "thorn in the flesh."

--2 Corinthians 12:8, "*For this thing I besought the Lord _____, that it might _____ from me.*"

Each time, God refused. God had a reason for making Paul continue to live with his discomfort. Notice the next verse:

--2 Corinthians 12:9, "*And He said unto me, My grace is _____ for thee: for _____ strength is made perfect in _____. Most gladly therefore will I rather glory in my _____, that the power of Christ may rest upon me.*"

In a sense, our addiction is our "*thorn in the flesh*". It most certainly works to keep us down. However, we must remember, just like Paul, God may not remove our "*thorn in the flesh.*" He may not completely take away our desire to use drugs and/or alcohol. We may continue to live with those desires. We do not have to act on our desires and remain in active addiction, but God wants us to remember how it feels to be in active addiction. This is so we can empathize with others. It may be God's plan for us to use our experiences to help others! It is possible God wants us to remember so we can share! We, too, can live with our *"thorn in the flesh"* just as Paul did!

DISCUSSION: **Besides addiction, name some other things that could be a "thorn in the flesh" in your life.** _____
_____
_____

There are still additional things I have trouble understanding. For instance, a group of teenagers are enjoying an afternoon canoeing on the river. An afternoon storm develops. The teenagers exit the river and are standing on the banks when a bolt of lightning strikes. One of the teenagers is killed by the lightning strike while the others are allowed to live. This one really happened in 1994. My seventeen-year-old brother was killed! He was my younger brother. My only brother. His friends lived, he died! They are still alive today. Try to make sense of that! It can't logically be done. This is the world in which we live. It's tough. At the very least, it is complex!

Time does indeed move on. Sometimes it feels as if we're left behind, but we're not. Time is one-dimensional, so therefore, it marches on. The only direction we can go is forward. We cannot go back! Sometimes we don't feel like going forward. It doesn't matter. We're headed that direction anyway. The hands of time still move in one direction and we are along for the ride. Time will continue to work this way until Jesus comes back. Then, time will be no longer.

--Revelation 10:6, *"And sware by Him that liveth for ever and ever, who created heaven, and the things that therein are, and the _____, and the things that therein are, and the _____, and the things which are therein, that there should be _____ no longer."*

But until then, we continue to plod through the doldrums of life.

I've tried to make sense of my own life on many occasions! I have never been able to completely do so. Even now, at some junctures, I fail to find peace. Some moments I have peace, other moments peace eludes me. I don't like the feeling of not having peace. I like the feeling of being peaceful, but finding true peace is difficult!

It's probable we feel the same way. We are human. We know about demons. You're familiar with your demons as I am familiar with mine. We likely feel that every demon known to mankind has crossed our path at some point! If we let them, they'll work against us to rob us of peace. We simply cannot let this happen. We have to fight! If we become over-confident, we set ourselves up for failure.

We must be careful or we fall prey to Satan!

--Ephesians 6:11, *"Put on the whole armour of God, that ye may be able to stand against the _____ of the _____."*

DEFINE "wiles." _____
_____
_____.

--1 Corinthians 10:12, *"Wherefore let him that thinketh he standeth take heed lest he _____."*

    For whatever reason, many of us have failed to live up to the expectations others had for us or we had for ourselves. We feel like we have failed and we feel this way often. Perhaps we haven't failed tremendously, but still, we have failed in some capacity. We cannot seem to forget. We're tired of feeling this way and we are looking for a better way to live!
    We don't like to acknowledge we have failed. We sure don't want to talk about it; at least much. So, we try to forget, but we can't. We look for anything that will help us survive from one day to the next. Oftentimes, we make the mistake of turning to drugs and/or alcohol to help us forget our failures.
    I made the mistake of using drugs for the first time at a young age. I've not used drugs all my life, but I've used them in stages. Drugs have never helped me accomplish anything! To the contrary, drugs have kept me from accomplishing a lot of the things I intended to accomplish!

DISCUSSION: Have you ever noticed a person lose something to drugs and/or alcohol? _____ **What was it?** _____
_____
_____

    I am over fifty years of age. I have fewer days ahead of me than I have behind me. As I look back over my life, I see a pattern. Perhaps you see a pattern in your life as well. In some stressful moments, I made the mistake of turning to drugs. I don't completely understand why, I just know I did, and I was wrong. Perhaps I did not want to experience a moment I was living in. Perhaps I did not want to remember details. We all have stressful moments. Stressful moments can include, job changes, moving from city-to-city, death of a loved one, marital problems, boredom, low self-esteem, financial failure, hurtful memories, legal issues, etc. During times such as these, we must remember nothing good will happen if we choose to use.
    It is a part of my personal recovery to help others find peace in their lives. Peace can be found through self-examination, reflection, and a study of God's Word. In addition, it is helpful for us to share our experiences with others. The hardest part of sharing is finding someone who'll listen. It may be difficult to find someone willing to listen. That's okay, keep looking.

--John 14:27, *"_____ I leave with you, My peace I give unto you: not as the _____ giveth, give I unto you. Let not your _____ be troubled, neither let it be _____."*

It is likely there are some reading this Study Guide who *are not* addicts (I hope so), and therefore do not understand the madness associated with the lifestyle of a user. I hope you will open your heart. I hope you will not give up on those struggling. I hope you will look for ways to be compassionate. Jesus was compassionate on more than one occasion.

--Matthew 14:14, *"And Jesus went forth, and saw a great multitude, and was moved with _____ toward them, and He healed their _____."*

--Matthew 20:34, *"So Jesus had _____ on them, and touched their eyes: and immediately their eyes received _____, and they followed Him."*

    The disease of addiction is a complex issue. We've heard said "knowledge is power." I wholeheartedly agree. When we have knowledge of how the disease of addiction works, we then have power to help ourselves or someone else.
    There are plenty of people in the world today looking for answers to questions about addiction. It is hard to find one family who does not have a member suffering from addiction. In addition, families also suffer and feel helpless and hopeless.
    Things will never be completely understood, at least, this side of Heaven. But there is a purpose, and anyone can find that purpose if he/she will seek a Higher Power. I might add, our purpose will never be found if we continue in our addiction. We must stop the insane cycle of using.
    I completely understand some believe in God, but are not religious. Still yet, others are religious but do not believe in God. We do not share the same spiritual views. That's okay. Look, we're still alive, we still have time, and we still have hope. Let's just agree to give God a try. We've nothing to lose and everything to gain!
    Yes, mistakes have been made. We are human and this happens. However, one thing I have learned, God does not make any mistakes and He made you and me!
    Addict or not, we are a lot alike. We're all together on this third rock from the sun! We'd all like to be better at making the most of the time we have. None of us wakes up wanting to be a failure. We are all looking for something better.
    As we look forward, let's agree to make as many good choices as we possibly can. Understand, mistakes will be made. Welcome to Life! However, with each mistake made, we have opportunity to learn. How we respond to each mistake determines our outlook on life! The more we learn, the better we are positioned to help others!
    Truth be known, we could all use a little help.

LESSON 2
"The Greatest of These is Love"
1 Corinthians 13:1-3

During my undergraduate studies I remember studying the approach and methods of Dr. Karl Meninger. He summarized a healthy life by his therapeutic approach stating that "Love is the medicine for the sickness of the world. Love cures. It cures those who give it and it cures those who receive it."

I have been blessed being married to my wonderful wife, Lisa, for twenty-nine years. I love her and she loves me. We have four wonderful children, ages 25, 21, 17, and 17. (We have identical twin girls)!

I haven't always been loveable. I've made plenty of mistakes. My using drugs at times during my married life has put a heavy strain on my marriage.

Fortunately, my wife has chosen to look beyond my mistakes. She has chosen to stay married to me because she loves me. She believes in me. She has helped me through some dark times. Times when I have been locked away in a jail cell or receiving treatment in a rehabilitation facility.

As a former addict, I can testify it was a struggle maintaining my addiction while attempting to show love. Drugs and/or alcohol worked together to numb my senses. It was hard to show love. It was hard to show love with chemicals in my bloodstream!

--2 Corinthians 4:4, "*In whom the god of this world hath _____ the minds of them which believe not, lest the _____ of the glorious gospel of Christ, who is the _____ of God, should shine unto them.*"

It's wrong to assume that addicts do not love because we most certainly do! The problem is, drugs and/or alcohol are so powerful, we are blinded. We cannot see how to love. Anyone close to an addict may falsely assume we do not have the capacity to love. This is a distorted view of an addict. Satan would love to blind us and keep us believing this way!

DISCUSSION: What persons have we failed to show love to while we were in active addiction? _____
What were we doing with our time that kept us from showing love to those closest to us? _____

What regrets do we have? _____

Many people undervalue the meaning of love. It's easy to love when things are going well. It's not so easy to love when life is turned upside-down. It is easy to give up and quit. Don't quit. Look for ways to love! Love truly is good medicine. It has been said that the three most powerful words in the English language are "I love you."

Many people do not understand love, and are even afraid of it, because they've never seen it done well. But even with all our counterfeits and misunderstanding, and even in spite of the abuses committed in the name of love, it is still true, love is a wonderful thing. Not just the word "love". We need the real thing. We need to see, hear, and feel love in our own lives. More importantly, we need to know how to pass it along to others.

1 Corinthians chapter 13 is oftentimes referred to, in the Bible, as the "Love Chapter". Many songs have been written from this chapter and this chapter is also read at weddings.

There are lots of ways to use the word "love" today. For instance, I love my wife. I love my four children. I love to go fishing. I love to golf. I love my biscuits dipped in chocolate gravy. The question is, what kind of love is the apostle Paul talking about in 1 Corinthians chapter 13?

To better understand this chapter, we need to know the four Greek words for love. They are as follows:

(1) <u>Eros</u> – this is sexual love. This is not used in the New Testament.

(2) <u>Storge</u> – this is friendly affection. This word is used in the New Testament for the warm affection that should exist between religious believers.

(3) <u>Philos</u> – this is family love. When joined with the Greek word "Adelphos" (brother), it means "Brotherly Love". This is how the city of Philadelphia got its name. It is used in the New Testament for our love for God and for others.

(4) <u>Agape</u> – this is self-sacrificing love. This word was rarely used before the New Testament period and uniquely describes God's love for us. Agape love is love that reaches out to another person with absolutely no strings attached. It is love that sacrifices itself on behalf of the one loved with no thought of what might be received in return.

This is the word Paul uses in 1 Corinthians chapter 13. It is love that starts with God, comes down to us, and then moves out from us to other people.

--1 Corinthians 13:1, "*Though I speak with the tongues of men and of angels, and have not _____ (love), I am become as sounding brass, or a tinkling cymbal.*"

Paul first tells us love is greater than eloquent communication. Have you tried to learn to speak a foreign language? It's not easy to do. I studied Spanish in high school and German in college. Along the way, I memorized long lists of words in each language. Apparently, it didn't do much good. I remember very little of the languages I studied so long ago. I have spent too much time watching westerns and golf, and not enough time working on my foreign languages. I speak English and that's basically it.

1 Corinthians 13:1 tells us without love it does not matter how many languages we speak or how eloquently we communicate our message. The greatest linguist in the world is ineffective if they speak without love.

Paul addressed the men of Athens. Paul was an apostle and spoke with love. Some of his listeners believed him.

--Acts 17:34, "Howbeit certain men clave unto him, and _____: among the which was Dionysius the Areopagite, and a woman named Damaris, and _____ with them."

If Paul had not loved, his message would have been ineffective. But it wasn't. It was powerful. Why? Paul had love. He preached Jesus, and people listened.

--Acts 17:31, "Because He hath appointed a _____, in the which He will _____ the world in righteousness by that man whom He hath ordained; whereof He hath given assurance unto all men, in that He hath raised Him from the _____."

To better understand the second part of 1 Corinthians 13:1, it is helpful to know some pagan religions of ancient Greece used loud cymbals to get the attention of their gods. Paul's message is clear in this verse. If we speak without love, we are no better than the pagans who do not even know God.

--1 Corinthians 13:2, "And though I have the gift of prophecy, and understand all _____, and all knowledge; and though I have all faith, so that I could remove _____, and have not _____ (love), I am nothing."

In verse two Paul tells us love is greater than spiritual gifts. In this verse, Paul mentions three spiritual gifts he had previously discussed in 1 Corinthians chapter 12.
    (1) <u>Prophecy</u> refers to the ability to declare God's truth as He has revealed it.
    (2) <u>Knowledge</u> involves the deep understanding of the Word of God.
    (3) <u>Faith</u> is the unique ability to trust God for great things at any time, and in any place.
    Yet Paul is saying without love these gifts are nothing.
    Let's suppose a person was so intelligent they were brilliant in math, science, history, language arts, and mechanics. Let's also suppose this same person was the most gifted speaker in the world. According to 1 Corinthians 13:2, God would say, "It's not enough!" Without love, the rest doesn't matter.
    When we are in active addiction, we need love! We need people to love us enough to help us achieve sobriety. Unfortunately, a lot of times, users don't let people help until a rock bottom has been reached!

--1 Corinthians 13:3, "And though I bestow all my goods to feed the _____, and though I give my body to be burned, and have not _____ (love), it profiteth me _____."

DISCUSSION: Addicts devote most of their time to their addiction. If you are an addict, or know an addict, what are some things that seem to matter most?
_____
_____
_____
_____

Paul moves on to say love is greater than personal sacrifice. Verse three poses a problem because it asks us to ponder activities, we automatically consider to be noble. Giving to the poor is a good thing and dying for your faith in Christ is the ultimate sacrifice. As good as these things are, without love, they are futile.

DEFINE "futile." _____
_____
_____

It would be great to be rich enough to give money to worthy causes. What if we were rich enough to guarantee every person on earth would have enough to eat and no one would ever go hungry? Wouldn't that be a wonderful thing to be able to do? It is sobering to understand Paul is telling us God says this is not enough. If we do give on a large scale, and we do it without love, nothing is gained. It truly would be great for the recipients, but nothing would be gained by the person who is giving, if they are giving without love!

The truth is, we may give to worthy causes for unworthy reasons. We may give out of guilt. We may give because we want to follow the crowd. We may give because we seek the praise of men. We may give for financial reasons. We may give to accomplish some other earthly goal. If we give for these reasons, the people on the receiving end will be blessed, but the giver will not.

DISCUSSION: What time in your life have you given to someone or something without giving in Love? _____
_____
_____

What was accomplished? _____
_____

--1 Corinthians 13:4-8, "_____ (love) suffereth long, and is kind; _____ (love) envieth not; _____ (love) vaunteth not itself, is not puffed up, (5) Doth not behave itself unseemly, seeketh not her own, is not easily _____, thinketh no evil; (6) Rejoiceth not in iniquity, but rejoiceth in the _____; (7) Beareth all things, believeth all things, hopeth all things, _____ all things. (8) _____ (love) never faileth: but whether there be prophecies, they shall fail; whether there be _____, they shall cease; whether there be knowledge, it shall _____ away."

It's hard for an addict to accomplish much, other than using. We start a lot of projects we rarely finish. We mean well. We just can't follow through with the good intentions of our heart because our brains are under the influence of powerful chemicals. We desperately need someone to love us and help us! Once again, it is difficult to succeed at recovery without love and support.

It's especially hard for an addict to love others because we rarely love ourselves. If we are to ever show love to someone else, we must first learn to love ourselves.

We can learn to do this. It is a process, and, it can be a painful one. But we can do it. We must do it. But how? First, we must make the decision, in our mind, that we are miserable in our addiction. We want to live again. We want to make others proud. We want to be proud of ourselves. We want to love ourselves. We want to love others. We want to do good. A journey of 1,000 miles begins with a first step. We need love to help us take the first step toward recovery. We need someone to love us in this way.

Our wives, husbands, daughters, sons, mothers, fathers, grandchildren, uncles, aunts, nieces, nephews, cousins, and friends watch to see if we take steps to get help. We will find, when we try to help ourselves, others are willing to help. But many times we disappoint by doing absolutely nothing to help ourselves. We only continue in our addiction!

If we truly want to be well, we must do whatever necessary to put some "sober time" between now and the next time we use.

During this sober time, we must place ourselves in an environment that makes acquiring drugs and/or alcohol difficult, if not impossible. The harder it is for us to acquire drugs and/or alcohol, the better off we are.

I must caution addicts and their families. There are unpleasant behaviors associated with attempting to quit drugs and/or alcohol. These are called withdrawal symptoms. Withdrawal symptoms include, but are not limited to, mental and physical aches. Experiencing these symptoms are a necessary part of the recovery process!

DISCUSSION: Have we failed to spend time with people we love because of an addiction? _____
Do we regret the lost opportunities? _____

If we are honest with ourselves, which is not easy in the best of circumstances, we must eventually admit we all have a long way to go in the area of love. Many of us struggle with difficult people and painful circumstances. When we have been deeply hurt by those closest to us, the temptation is often overwhelming to respond with anger, bitterness, and hatred. In our desperation it is easy to sink to the level of those who have betrayed our trust. We let our pain develop into madness. Being an addict, we return to using. This is not a good thing. This is devastating. We start the process of recovery over again. We once again hurt people. We must once again try to forgive ourselves. Love is hard. Loving ourself is harder.

--Proverbs 26:11, "*As a dog returneth to his _____, so a _____ returneth to his folly.*"

Jesus embodied God's love and His own people crucified Him.

--Matthew 27:41-43, "*Likewise also the chief priests mocking Him, with the _____ and _____, said, (42) He saved others; Himself He cannot _____. If He be the King of Israel, let Him now come down from the _____, and we will believe Him. (43) He trusted in God; let Him deliver Him now, if He will have Him: for He said, I am the Son of _____.*"

Sobriety is the offspring of love. When we desire to love, the idea of sobriety becomes achievable! Love isn't about us. Love is about God. Since God is love, all true love starts with Him and comes down to us.

--1 John 4:7-8, "*Beloved, let us _____ one another: for love is of God; and every one that loveth is born of God, and knoweth God. (8) He that loveth not knoweth not God; for God is _____.*"

If we want to be more loving, we must get to know God better. We get to know God better through the study of His Word and putting His Word into action. As we come to know the God of love in a personal way, His love will supernaturally flow through us as our hearts and minds are transformed.

--Romans 12:2, "*And be not conformed to this world: but be ye _____ by the renewing of your mind, that ye may prove what is that good, and acceptable, and perfect, will of _____.*"

Jesus is proof of God's love. Look at the cross. There we see God's love made real. Through His sacrifice, Jesus Christ has stayed our execution. The bells of Hell will never toll for faithful Christians.

God loves each of us. May we do whatever it takes to put ourselves in a position to love Him back. If you are in active addiction, care enough about yourself to let God help. Care enough about your family to let God help. There are places you can go right away for help. Email this author and I will help any way I can. Why wait any longer?

DISCUSSION: Why do you feel it is hard for an addict to ask for help?
_____
_____
_____
_____

--John 3:16, "*For God so loved the world, that He gave His only begotten _____, that whosoever believeth in Him should not perish, but have everlasting _____.*"

--James 4:14, "*Whereas ye know not what shall be on the morrow. For what is your life? It is even a _____, that appeareth for a little _____, and then vanisheth away.*"

Something must be done while we have opportunity. We are not promised one more minute here on earth!

If you're an addict, ask for help! Let God help you! Let other people help you!

If you have a loved-one or friend in active addiction, please help any way you can!

LESSON 3
"Our Guide for Hard Times"
James 1:1-4

A recent news article disclosed overdosing from fentanyl was the number one cause of death in people ages 18-49! The article went on to point out 195 Americans died every single day in 2021 due to this lethal drug. There's no doubt the numbers are higher today; staggering, sad, and pitiful. Nevertheless, we continue to "roll the dice" and use. We want to stop, but we can't. We're exhausted, but we continue flirting with death.

We live in dangerous times. Does anyone doubt it? COVID-19 has been on the scene for the last few years. School shootings seem to be happening more frequently. We are being desensitized to violence!

Things do not shock us like they should. Some people can't figure out which bathroom to use. In some parts of the world biological men are participating in women's sports. We are being warned artificial intelligence could take over the world. Wars are raging in distant countries and we pay little attention. People are living in boxes in the United States and little help is offered, while billions of dollars in aid is being sent to foreign governments. We struggle to make our world make any sense! It's no wonder we use drugs and/or alcohol! This world has lost its way!

DISCUSSION: Name some things that would have shocked us thirty years ago but do not shock us today. _____
_____
_____

We are all in harm's way. Trouble is all around us. Notice what Job has to say:

--Job 5:7, *"Yet man is born unto _____, as the sparks fly upward."*

--Job 14:1, *"Man that is born of a woman is of few days and full of _____."*

I see no way to deny those statements. They were true thousands of years ago and remain true today. We are a troubled people living on a troubled planet.

Because we live in a fallen, unpredictable world, nothing works the way it's supposed to. Sin has stained every part of our universe. To some extent, we adults are to blame. We've done wrong while knowing what is right!

--Romans 3:23, *"For all have _____, and come short of the glory of God."*

When Adam drove the bus of humanity off the cliff, we all went with him.

--Romans 5:12, *"Wherefore, as by _____ man sin entered into the world, and _____ by sin; and so death passed upon all men, for that all have _____."*

13

Our bodies wear out. We grow old and die. People kill each other. Marriages break up. Adults and children get hooked on drugs, alcohol, and much more! Babies are born with defects that cannot be corrected. Our leaders disappoint us. Our friends turn into our enemies.

It's no wonder we cannot find peace. I wish drugs didn't exist, but they do, and I understand why people use them. Our minds are racing. We can't slow down. Is the news really fake? How can any of us truly know? Our brains hurt. We are looking for something certain, truthful, and helpful. We can't seem to find what we're looking for, so we turn to using. Wrong move! Big mistake!

--John 17:17, "*Sanctify them through thy _____: thy _____ is truth.*"

These are difficult days in many parts of the world. I believe more hard times are coming to Christians worldwide.

We, as Christians, need to know how to survive as our culture develops a less tolerable attitude toward us.

Though the book of James is the earliest of all New Testament books (written around A.D. 38-44), it reads like a letter for us today.

--James 1:1, "*James, a servant of God and of the Lord Jesus Christ, to the _____ tribes which are scattered _____, greeting.*"

Here is what we need to know about the book of James and its author:

(1) James was evidently the half-brother of Jesus, meaning he was the biological son of Joseph and Mary.

(2) We know he wrote very early because the book is addressed to the "*twelve tribes scattered abroad*". This meant James was seeking to address the very earliest Jewish believers who had been scattered due to the persecution of the church in Jerusalem. The verse below addresses this issue.

(3) Those early Christians were Jewish, scattered, poor, and struggling.

(4) In many ways, the letter of James is the most practical book in the New Testament. It reads like a pep-talk!

In the following verse we see Luke, the writer of Acts, reaffirm what James wrote concerning Christians being "scattered".

--Acts 8:1, "*And Saul was consenting unto his _____. And at that time there was a great _____ against the _____ which was at _____; and they were all _____ abroad throughout the regions of Judaea and Samaria, except the _____.*"

When we read the book of James, we get a glimpse of Christianity in its earliest form. No theory, just straight talk from Jesus' half-brother about what works and what doesn't work in the Christian life.

There are over fifty commands found in the five chapters of James! James begins with an exhortation (urging) about how to respond when hard times come. After 2,000 years, his words still have meaning for us today because hard times still exist!

DISCUSSION: Name some ways that Christians feel persecuted today.
_____
_____
_____

--James 1:2, "*My brethren, count it all _____ when ye fall into _____ temptations...*"

    James begins by reminding us sooner or later we will all face trials of various sorts. No matter who we are, or where we live, trouble is all around us. Trouble is just a phone call away, or a conversation away. A doctor may come in and say, "I'm sorry. You've got cancer." The voice on the phone may inform us our son or daughter has just been arrested. We may be fired from our employment without warning. Someone we trusted may start spreading lies about us. Our spouse may decide he/she does not want to be married any longer. The list is endless because our struggles are endless. We look for some relief. We feel we cannot deal with reality any longer!

    In times such as these, it is important to remember drugs and /or alcohol will not solve our problems. They've never solved our problems before. Why would we think they'll start now? They'll only work to create new problems. The hammer falls hard! Many of us have tried the "chemical" escape route. It does not work. Why not try something new? Why don't we let God help this time? Why not give God a try?

    James offers what appears to be a strange piece of advice. He says to "*count it all joy*" when struggles come our way! That sounds so odd we wonder if he is serious. It does sound rather idealistic, if not impossible. "*Counting it all joy*" when trouble comes is not a natural human response.

    If we want a natural human response to struggles, we can talk about anger, despair, lying, bitterness, complaining, getting even, running away, or using drugs and/or alcohol. It isn't natural to find joy in hardship. But that's the whole point. James isn't talking about a natural human reaction. He is telling us we have a conscious decision to make when we are experiencing hard times. We should try to make the choice to find joy. A joy that comes from knowing no matter how difficult the struggle is, God will help us through.

    God will help us through our addiction, but we must let Him! We have to give up things we think are important. Do it! Let God work in your life for a while! As addicts, we've done nothing but make a mess of it all. Stop making a mess and let God help clean it up!

DISCUSSION: What do you think Psalm 46:10 means when it says, "*Be still, and know that I am God...*" _____
_____
_____

--1 Corinthians 10:13, "*There hath no _____ taken you but such as is common to _____: but God is faithful, who will not suffer you to be _____ above that ye are able; but will with the temptation also make a way to _____, that ye may be able to _____ it.*"

Words are useless without action! We should simply not trust our feelings when we are using! Truth is, during active addiction, we rarely know what we are feeling!

When those we love are in great pain or when we face senseless tragedy or when friends turn against us or when life tumbles in around us, our feelings are never going to be an accurate guide, especially if we are under the influence.

No doubt, our main problem comes because we misunderstand the word "joy". To most of us the word "joy" means the absence of all pain. That is not what the Bible means. "Joy" is a deep satisfaction that comes from knowing God is in control even when our circumstances seem to be out of control.

For many of us, our circumstances seem to be out of control quite often. Things are out of control because we are using. Stop the madness! Try making a conscious effort to grow closer to God during these times. When we do, we'll discover the power of God! What do we have to lose? Nothing! When we let God be in control, we can find peace at a very deep level even while we weep over what is happening all around us.

--Philippians 4:7, "And the _____ of God, which passeth all understanding, shall keep your _____ and _____ through Christ Jesus."

--James 1:3, "Knowing this, that the _____ of your faith worketh _____."

In the verse directly above, James gives us a reason to turn to God during the hardships of our life. Every word of this verse is crucial. The word "trying" (testing) refers to the process by which gold ore was purified. In order to separate the gold from the dross (rubbish), the ore was placed in a furnace and heated until it melted. The dross (rubbish) rose to the surface and was skimmed off, leaving only pure gold.

Job speaks of this process:

--Job 23:10, "But He knoweth the way that I take: when He hath tried me, I shall come forth as _____."

This is a picture of what God is doing during our fiery trials. If you are in active addiction, you are in the middle of a fiery trial. We all have to undergo some furnace time sooner or later. Some of us will spend an extended amount of time in the furnace of affliction. But we should take comfort knowing eventually the result will be the pure gold of a Christ-like character shining forth in our lives.

This is exactly what we're looking for! Let's put all the bad behavior associated with addiction behind us! When we do this, we will notice an improvement, and others will too.

Until our faith is put to the test, it remains only theoretical. We never know what we believe until struggles come our way. When our phone rings with bad news, when our son or daughter winds up in prison, when our best friend betrays us, when we lose our jobs, when our parents suddenly die, when life comes apart at the seams, then, we discover what we truly believe!

Until then, our faith is speculative because it is untested! We have to know struggles before we can appreciate the true power of God.

We can talk about Heaven all we want, but we'll discover whether or not we truly believe in it when we stand beside the casket of someone we love or watch a loved one suffer terrible pain before their death.

DISCUSSION: Name some people you love who have passed away. _____

How did you cope with their deaths? _____
_____
_____
_____

--Revelation 14:12, "*Here is the _____ of the saints: here are they that keep the _____ of God, and the faith of Jesus.*"

Primarily, the New Testament was originally written in Greek. The Greek word for "patience" is sometimes translated as "perseverance" or "steadfastness". In the book of Revelation, this word describes the faith of those brave saints who would not take the mark of the beast. The verse above gives us an example of a battle-tested faith that stands up under fire. We all need a battle-tested faith because the devil seeks to do battle with us every single day. Each time we think of using, we are at battle with the devil!

--1 Peter 5:8, "*Be _____, be vigilant; because your adversary the _____, as a roaring lion, walketh about, seeking whom he may _____.*"

--James 4:7, "*Submit yourselves therefore to God. Resist the _____, and he will _____ from you.*"

--James 1:4, "*But let _____ have her perfect work, that ye may be perfect and entire (complete), wanting (lacking) _____.*"

There is a process involved in our struggles that leads to a product. Many of us can attest to the fact we are stronger Christians today as a result of struggles we've faced over the course of our lives. Patience and perseverance require desperate dependence and stubborn determination to hold on to our faith, even when the world seems to disintegrate around us.

Perseverance says, "I will not give up regardless of what happens or how bad life may be. I will hold on because I know God has something in store for me."

That sort of gritty stubbornness produces genuine spiritual maturity. When struggles have finished their work in us, we will not lack anything the Lord desires for us to have. If we need faith, we will have it. If we need hope, we will have it. If we need love, we will have it. If we need any of the fruits of the Spirit, they will be produced in us.

--Galatians 5:22-23, *"But the fruit of the Spirit is love, joy, peace, longsuffering, gentleness, goodness, faith, (23) Meekness, temperance: against such there is no _____."*

When trials come, and they come to all of us eventually, there is something we can't know and something we can know.

We <u>can't always know</u> why things happen the way they do. No matter how hard we try to figure things out, there will always be many mysteries in life. The greater the tragedy, the greater the mystery. God does not explain Himself to us. As we go through life, we can look back and see many blanks we wish God would fill in for us. Most of the time we carry those unfilled blanks with us all the way to the grave, and eventually, to Heaven.

Job tried to solicit answers from God and God responded in the following way:

--Job 38:4, *"Where wast thou when I laid the foundations of the _____? Declare, if thou hast understanding."*

God asked Job where Job was when God created the foundations of the earth. In other words, God was telling Job that He did not need Job's help in doing His work.

Many times, we make the mistake of wanting to help God do His work. We must remember, however, that God is God, and we are not!

We <u>can know</u> there is an abundant life, spiritual victory, and joy in the Lord. Those things do not come in spite of our trials. Most often they come through, and alongside our trials.

In various ways we struggle every day as we make our earthly journey. In a fallen world there can be no other way. For the most part, we can't choose our struggles nor can we avoid them. But we can choose how we respond. That part is up to us.

Our perspective makes all the difference and this is what James is telling us in our lesson text. God does not intend to destroy us by the trials He allows to come our way.

Things that seem so painful now will one day be clearly seen as being beneficial to our spiritual growth. They are not meant to defeat us, but rather, to strengthen us.

Therefore, we should not complain when hard times come. Rather, we should try to rejoice. We will rejoice when we believe what God has said.

If we are in active addiction at the moment, let's try to rejoice! Why? Because when we achieve sobriety, we will be stronger than ever!

Every struggle is a step on the stairway that leads from Earth to Heaven.

Remember, there is purpose in your struggle with addiction. There are better things waiting for you on the other side of addiction!

LESSON 4
"We Are Our Own Worst Enemy"
2 Corinthians 1:3-11

If we are totally honest with ourselves, most of the problems we experience in life are a direct result of poor choices we make. We choose to go out with the wrong crowd. We participate in activities that aren't healthy. We experiment with drugs and/or alcohol. After a period of time, our lives are in disarray and we are left looking in the mirror wondering what went wrong. In short, the answer is, we have gone wrong. It is our fault! We have chosen to use drugs and/or alcohol. We have sown something bad. The apostle Paul tells us we will reap what we have sown.

--Galatians 6:7, *"Be not _____; God is not _____: for whatsoever a man soweth, that shall he also reap."*

We get back what we've given. We lie, steal, cheat, and deceive. We give bad things and get bad things in return. It takes hitting rock bottom before many of us can begin putting the pieces of our lives back together again. Some of us never complete the puzzle; but we try. That's what's important. We keep trying. We should never quit trying! There is always hope tomorrow will be a better day!

Sometimes decisions lead us down paths we never intended to follow. Life is hard. During our active addiction phases, we experience things that always remain with us. We rarely see this coming! We are blindsided. We didn't sign up for this! Some situations I have found myself in continue to break my heart, even today. I've learned to live with the heartache.

From time-to-time, I think of things I've seen, and wonder why I've seen them. I can't forget what I've seen. I wish I could. I chose to do drugs at different times in my life and the consequence have always been real and negative.

DISCUSSION: **Talk about times in your life when something bad happened while you were under the influence of drugs and/or alcohol.** _____
_____
_____
_____
_____

I suppose I've used about every drug available on the street. I'm not proud of this, but it has given me a perspective which I otherwise would not have. For this I'm thankful. I'm now in a position to help others overcome struggles with addiction. Without my periods of active addiction this would not be possible.

Throughout the course of my life, I've lost several friends and family members to drugs and/or alcohol. Some died from direct overdoses. Others died from accidents that happened while under the influence. I think about these occasionally and I can only shake my head. What a tragedy! What a loss! Losing friends and family prematurely to drugs and/or alcohol helps me put my own life in perspective.

One conclusion I've drawn is I'm not ready to die yet. Another conclusion is when it is my time to die, I certainly do not want to die under the influence of drugs and/or alcohol! I want to die sober! Thinking this way helps me to remain sober. Those in active addiction should pause and consider this for a moment. How do you want your family and friends to remember you when you're gone? Do you want them to remember you as being someone who died in their addiction?

I think of my family more now than ever. I choose to stay sober because I want to die sober! I do not want to die in my addiction!

DISCUSSION: How many people do you personally know, who directly, or indirectly, lost their lives as a result of drugs? _____
_____
_____

I have stories concerning addiction and death I intend to tell over time. I try to wait for the situations to be right. When talking about the dead, I never name names. To me, naming names shows disrespect for the dead. I only discuss these things now for therapeutic reasons. Sharing these stories is good for me. It's not healthy to keep things bottled-up inside. Communication is helpful in achieving, and maintaining sobriety. If we can learn to talk about our experiences, we are moving in the right direction. The key is, finding someone who cares enough to listen.

It hurts me to think about friends and family who have passed away. It breaks my heart to know their lives ended so suddenly, tragically, and abruptly.

I have several friends who have died from fentanyl overdoses. Two of the deaths immediately come to mind when I think about overdosing. Both were great guys. Both would give the shirt off their back to someone in need. Both came from good families. Both of their families were absolutely devastated at the news of their death. Both were found dead in their bedroom floors. Both had been dead long enough that Narcan would not work. Both were relatively young and had their whole life ahead of them. Neither intended to die the last time they used fentanyl; few people do. We know it can happen. We just think it will happen to someone else and not us. That's a tragic and deadly line of thinking.

I think about both quite often. I ask myself, why am I still living? I wonder why their lives ended and mine hasn't.

I have more friends who have died as a result of fentanyl than from all other drugs, combined. Cocaine, heroin, and benzodiazepines have claimed the lives of a few of my friends, but fentanyl, by far, is the deadliest drug I know.

I have scars on my arms and legs. I look at them every day. It's hard remembering where we've been! It's hard reliving the moments! It hurts.

Addiction leaves us with more questions than answers. I cannot make sense of it all. God knows I've used too much of one drug at a time. I keep looking for answers, knowing I may not find them. All I can say is "today, I'm riding the sober train. It has left the station and I am not looking for it to be derailed."

--Deuteronomy 29:29, "The _____ things belong unto the Lord our God: but those things which are revealed belong unto us and to our children for ever, that we may do all the words of this law."

--2 Corinthians 1:3-4, "Blessed be God, even the Father of our Lord Jesus Christ, the Father of _____, and the God of all _____; (4) Who comforteth us in all our _____ that we may be able to comfort them which are in any _____, by the comfort wherewith we ourselves are comforted of God."

    I acknowledge my problem with addiction could have been avoided if I would have made better choices. But I didn't. I chose to use. No one forced me. I cannot rewind the hands of time and change anything now. It's all in the past. Just as the apostle Paul pressed on, I too, press on.
    What I can do is stay sober today; one day at a time. I can wake up each day and make the decision to stay sober for that day. We can all do this! We must be careful not to promise to stay sober for a week, month, or year. That's too much! That's too much at one time! We need to stay sober one day at a time.

--Philippians 3:13-14, "Brethren, I count not myself to have apprehended: but this one thing I do, _____ those things which are behind, and reaching forth unto those things which are before, (14) I _____ toward the mark for the prize of the high calling of God in Christ Jesus."

DISCUSSION: What might Paul have wanted to forget? _____
_____

Hint: It concerns the early church.

    No one promises staying sober is going to be easy. We need God to help direct our paths.

--Proverbs 3:5-6, "Trust in the Lord with all thine _____; and lean not unto thine _____ understanding. (6) In all they ways acknowledge Him, and He shall direct thy _____."

    We have certain things in our lives that cause us to think about using. These are called triggers. Triggers can be people, places, things, emotions, etc. We should avoid these when possible! We try to forget drugs and/or alcohol but our minds and bodies work against us to cause us to remember times of active addiction as being good times. This is a lie! Triggers can cause a former addict to relapse if great caution is not taken. I have triggers in my life. Triggers can be as unique as addicts. We should identify and avoid things in our environment that cause us to think about using.

DEFINE "relapse." _____
_____

Before we actually use again, we think about using. After the thought, comes the action. The fewer thoughts we have of using, the better off we are!

DISCUSSION: What are some triggers in your life? _____
_____
_____

--2 Corinthians 1:5-6, *"For as the _____ of Christ abound in us, so our consolation also aboundeth by Christ. (6) And whether we be _____, it is for your _____ and _____, which is effectual in the enduring of the same sufferings which we also suffer: or whether we be _____, it is for your consolation and salvation."*

If we think we've suffered much in our addiction, think of how Christ suffered for us as a substitute. As we seek to be more sober and Christ-like, we should occasionally expect affliction. However, it will never be to the extent that Christ suffered. This is exactly what Paul is meaning in the verses above. Notice also what Peter says:

--1 Peter 2:21, *"For even hereunto were ye _____: because Christ also _____ for us, leaving us an _____, that ye should follow his _____."*

--2 Corinthians 1:1-2, *"Paul, an apostle of Jesus Christ by the will of God, and Timothy our brother, unto the church of God which is at _____, with all the saints which are in all Achaia: (2) _____ be to you and _____ from God our Father, and from the Lord Jesus Christ."*

After a brief greeting to his readers in verses 1-2 above, in which Paul wishes grace and peace to his readers in Corinth and throughout the surrounding region, he immediately begins to talk about the comfort he received in the middle of a hardship he endured as an apostle. In 2 Corinthians 1:3-11 Paul sets the stage for the entire epistle by saying no matter how much he had suffered, it was more than worth it.

We too, as addicts, need to make it to a place where we can truly say whatever happened to us, it was worth it. It was worth it because we now see just how fortunate we are to be alive. It was worth it because we now have knowledge to help someone who is struggling in their addiction!

As terrible as it was for us to use, it is better now because we are sober and alive! If you're not sober, you can be! It's a lifestyle you can attain! Maybe not right away, but it's not far away. It's possible. All things are possible with God! Notice the words of Jesus:

--Mark 10:27, *"And Jesus looking upon them saith, "With men it is _____, but not with God: for with God all things are _____.""*

DISCUSSION: Based on the above scripture, do you truly believe overcoming addiction is possible? _____
_____
_____

It's not so much what happens to us, it's how we react. It's about being a student of God rather than a victim of life! A victim says, "Why did this happen to me?" A student says, "What can I learn from this?"

A victim believes God abandoned them. A student sees God's hand in everything, including the worst moments of life. Paul tells us as much in the following verse:

--Romans 8:28, *"And we know that _____ things work together for _____ to them that love God, to them who are the called according to His _____."*

As we overcome addiction, we become relaxed and confident. Overcoming addiction helps us to clarify our priorities. Things that used to be important to us no longer matter. Things that used to have little value to us suddenly become valuable.

As mentioned in a previous lesson, as we struggle to overcome addiction, it is important to remember people are watching!

--Romans 14:7, *"For none of us _____ to himself, and no man _____ to himself."*

Our friends, family, and enemies watch to see how we respond to addiction-related struggles in our life.

People who do not understand addiction will ask questions such as, "Why don't they just get tough?", or "Why don't they show some backbone?", or "Why don't they quit complaining and get on with life?", or "Why can't they be strong like the rest of us?"

Our addiction has brought us to our knees. While on our knees we do not need to waste time wondering why some people do not understand us.

The only thing that matters is for us to remain sober! Some of us have been forced all the way to the ground. It's hard to get up! But let these times work in our favor. Let God help us back up. If we don't let God help us, there is a chance we won't get back up!

DISCUSSION: Name a time in your life when you have failed yourself, or others. Be brutally honest. _____
_____
_____
_____
_____

We are our own worst enemy because we do not pray enough! Many times, we view prayer as a last resort, when it ought to be our first action.

I've been guilty of this on occasions. It's a daily challenge for me to pray as I should. I continue to work on my prayer life. I try to pray before I go to bed, when I wake up, and at times during the day. I try to remember through prayer we unleash the power of Heaven to help us face the problems on earth.

As we receive comfort and strength through prayer, we are equipped to minister to others. We then pass along to others what God has given to us. This is the very essence of being a Christian.

--James 5:16, *"Confess your _____ one to another, and pray one for another, that ye may be healed. The effectual fervent _____ of a righteous man availeth _____."*

Have you ever gone to a pond and thrown a small rock into the water? What happens? From the point where the rock enters the water, ripples spread out. What starts as a ripple from one small rock soon affects the entire pond. That's a picture of what God wants to do in your life through prayer.

God comforts us in our trials so we might comfort another, who may comfort another, who may comfort another, and so on. The ripple effect of prayer may spread out from us to people we may never meet!

Addiction does cause many problems in life. But with God's help, we can overcome addiction and be the person He wants us to be. Don't waste your pain. Don't waste your struggles. Don't waste your hardships. Don't waste your experiences. Use them to grow closer to God. Also, use your pain, struggles, hardships, and experiences to minister to others. Pray more and do not keep things inside. Don't be your own worst enemy!

LESSON 5
"Choose to be Optimistic"
Ephesians 5:15-17

When we are living in active addiction, we are oblivious to other people's emotions. We hurt those we love. We lose the trust of those closest to us by being untruthful, unpredictable, hateful, and shallow. We treat our family and friends as enemies. We lash out at those trying to help us. We are unpleasant to be around. When we have a moment of sobriety, we remember these things. Our addiction weighs heavy on our heart.

When we are using, we are rarely given the benefit of any doubt. Why should we? We haven't exactly earned many awards for being truthful. So, what happens? If something is wrong, it's our fault. If something is missing, we must be guilty of taking it. If something doesn't work, we tore it up. Sometimes these things are true. Sometimes they're not. It's easy for us to throw our hands up in the air and quit. We feel as if we cannot win. To be honest, we've lied for so long we wouldn't know the truth if it slapped us in the face. We can't remember enough to know what truth is. While in active addiction we cannot expect others to believe us when we cannot believe ourselves!

Some addicts do illegal things to support their habits. Some steal. Some lie. Some deceive. However, some do not. All addicts should not be put in the same category, but oftentimes we are. This is frustrating.

In addition, when using, we associate with people we normally wouldn't associate with. This never ends well. We do things we normally wouldn't do. If we are careful, we are only careful to not get caught using. Getting caught means we go to jail, and, most usually, going to jail means we spend some time without drugs and/or alcohol. In other words, the gig is up, at least temporarily. To an addict, this is devastating because our bodies have developed chemical dependencies. We feel we have to use. We also greatly fear the withdrawal process.

While we are incarcerated, we think about using. We spend a great amount of time thinking about the next time we'll be able to use. We also think about our families, but not as much as using. We think about what we did to get caught and vow to never make that mistake again. The thought process of an addict is drastically different from someone who does not use drugs and/or alcohol. That is the nature of the addiction beast!

To an addict, there is no worse feeling than being without drugs and/or alcohol. Our bodies hurt. Our minds hurt. We do the best we can to survive the withdrawal process. We need to use to keep our bodies from hurting. We are in pain and can't think logically. We only want to use again. An addict's view of life during active addiction is grossly skewed. It seems we have few reasons to be optimistic!

DISCUSSION: **What things does an addict look forward to during active addiction?** _____
_____
_____

Many ride the carousel of addiction over and over and over again. To a sober person, it's insanity! To an addict, it is life. As hard as we may try, we cannot stop. We use more. We care less. We're not happy. We're miserable. We give up and stop trying to quit because we have tried stopping many times and failed each time. We simply quit trying to stop using. At this point, we plunge into a deep, dark place.

I have been in this place. It's a place of mental and physical anguish. It is a paradox. My mind knows I must quit using in order to live, but my body says I must use to live. My body wins this war! In chemical addiction there is no "mind over matter." About as close as addicts come to "mind over matter" is "if you don't mind, I'll use my drugs and/or alcohol because they're all that matters."

Paul offers three key pieces of advice in Ephesians 5:15-17 that will help us to achieve, and maintain sobriety.

--Ephesians 5:15-17, *"See then that ye walk circumspectly, not as _____, but as _____." (16) Redeeming the _____, because the days are _____. (17) Wherefore be ye not _____, but understanding what the _____ of the Lord is."*

The first thing the apostle Paul says is, if we want to succeed, we must watch our step. This is true in many different ways. As addicts looking to gain sobriety, we must be careful. God has given each of us a brain. He expects us to use it. If we are looking for sobriety, we will not find it in a group of active addicts! We must stay away from people in active addiction! This is one way we can *"walk circumspectly."* We must be careful where we go and with whom we associate!

--1 Corinthians 15:33, *"Be not _____: evil communications (companionships) corrupt _____ manners."*

DISCUSSION: **Think of times when you were around people with whom you should not have been. Did you use drugs and/or alcohol during these times?** _____
Was this a wise choice? _____
_____
_____
_____

"Walking circumspectly" has the idea of walking on a narrow path along the side of a steep mountain. We must keep our eyes open because if we take the wrong step we may plunge to our death.

When we don't watch where we are going, we are likely to trip and fall because we are not walking carefully. When we pay attention to people we associate with and places we go, we are much more likely to avoid triggers that work to lead us back into active addiction. When we make a decision to remain sober, we are doing our best to stay alive. Remaining alive depends on our dedication to walking carefully.

The second thing Paul says to do is to *"redeem the time"*. The particular reason Paul gives for "redeeming the time" is *"because the days are evil."* We too, live in evil days. It seems as if every person is doing what is right in their own eyes, with no regard for God's Word. We must be cautious because God knows our hearts and intents.

--Proverbs 21:2, *"Every way of a man is right in his own _____: but the Lord pondereth the _____."*

Paul writes the words in our text to the church in Ephesus while in a Roman jail. The emperor was a man by the name of Nero. Nero was a perverted excuse for a king. Nero set fire to Rome and blamed the Christians for it. Later, Nero orders Paul beheaded.

In Paul's day, Ephesus was the most important city in the Roman province of Asia. Located near the coast, Ephesus served as a center for international commerce. It was a prosperous and sinful city. Attempting to spread God's Word in Paul's day seemed like a losing battle. That's why Paul says the times were desperate!

Today, our world has a lot in common with Ephesus. Evil days tempt us to despair. We are tempted to use drugs and/or alcohol. We are told we may do whatever feels right. Evil days tempt us to want to give up. Don't give up! Choose to be optimistic because God is in control! He'll help us through these times. God will help us achieve sobriety!

The third thing Paul says to do is *"Do God's Will."* We *"Do God's Will"* by studying, praying, and letting Him lead us.

We must study the Bible, pray for God to help us understand His Word, and let God guide our path to sobriety. If we ask, He will help us!

--Jeremiah 10:23, *"O Lord, I know that the way of _____ is not in himself: it is not in man that walketh to direct his _____."*

--Isaiah 41:10, *"Fear thou not; for I am with thee: be not _____; for I am thy God: I will _____ thee; yea, I will _____ thee; yea, I will uphold thee with the right hand of my righteousness."*

On resurrection Sunday, as the truth slowly dawned that Jesus had risen from the dead, despair gave way to hope. Pessimism turned to optimism! As believers in God, we are both pessimists and optimists. However, we are much more optimistic because, when we are sober, we can see what is happening in the world around us and know everything will be okay, because Jesus left behind an empty tomb!

Even though we may struggle with addiction, God is here to help us. In the end, if we are believers, we have hope of maintaining sobriety and knowing eternal life.

LESSON 6
"Overcoming Failure"
Luke 22:54-65

The price of addiction is high. Oftentimes, it's more than we were expecting to pay. Families, jobs, reputations, motivation, self-esteem, friendships, and lives are some of the things lost to the high price of addiction.

Some things are lost and never regained. It is difficult to mend every broken relationship. We apologize. We try to make amends. We cry, if we can. We accept the fact we have failed. We put our best foot forward. We move on. This is all we can do.

Achieving sobriety requires us to end relationships with certain people. We should end relationships with those who are using. Simply put, there are people with whom we should not associate. There are also times we'll need to end relationships with those who *are not* using. There are people who possess spirits of unforgiveness and negativity! We should avoid such people! Addiction works this way. We can be close to a person one day and far away the next. We must do what is best for us! We know ourselves better than anyone else does.

While struggling, we learn some people cannot look beyond our addiction. In addition, we learn we aren't nearly as valuable to people as we once thought.

We must accept we are a failure in the eyes of some. There are those who no longer trust us. There are those who do not want to be around us. There are those who treat us as if we no longer exist. We are shunned. We are treated as second-class citizens. To an addict, this is reality, and a hard pill to swallow!

We must not let reality stand in the way of our recovery! We must quit putting ourselves in positions to be treated unkindly. Even on a good day, the level of difficulty in achieving sobriety is off the charts. Even on a day when people treat us kindly it is hard to stay sober! When we are treated unkindly it makes for a most difficult day. Achieving sobriety is a difficult thing to do. Maintaining sobriety is just as hard as achieving sobriety. We must stay away from those who treat us with disdain and intolerance! We cannot afford to wait around for every person to treat us kindly. This will never happen! We must move on!

We must do as Jesus told the disciples to do. We must shake the dust off our feet and move on; keep traveling. Full speed ahead!

--Matthew 10:14, *"And whosoever shall not _____ you, nor hear your _____, when ye depart out of that house or city, shake off the _____ of your feet."*

We must be willing to start life anew from where we are today. If we are sober today, we must remain sober today, while intending to stay sober tomorrow.

--Matthew 18:21-22, *"Then came Peter to Him, and said, Lord, how oft shall my brother sin against me, and I _____ him? Till seven times? (22) Jesus saith unto him, I say not unto thee, until _____ times: but, Until seventy _____ seven."*

DISCUSSION: We are to forgive those who sin against us. In the above two verses Jesus points out that forgiveness should be unlimited when true repentance is present. Does this exclude those who are struggling with addiction? _____. Why? _____
_____
_____
_____

    We must make peace with our past failures. We must be willing to push forward, acknowledging we have failed.
    We can learn a lesson about overcoming failures from the apostle Peter. It happened one Friday morning in Jerusalem. A rooster crowed and Peter never forgot it. In fact, it was written down in the Bible four different times by Matthew (26:69-75), Mark (14:66-72), Luke (22:54-65), and John (18:15-27). In this story the apostle Peter falls and gets up again.
    What Peter did is exactly what we must do. We have fallen and we must get back up! As an addict, we have failed. We have fallen. We never intended to become addicted, but we must accept reality! It is not easy!
    The other apostles had scattered, leaving only Peter. The other apostles were shocked and angry by the actions of Judas. Judas is the apostle that sold Jesus for thirty pieces of silver.

--Matthew 26:14-15, *"Then one of the _____, called Judas Iscariot, went unto the chief priests, (15) And said unto them, What will ye give me, and I will _____ Him unto you? And they covenanted with him for _____ pieces of silver."*

    As the soldiers led Jesus away, Peter decides to follow. He had promised earlier to never desert Jesus.

--Matthew 26:33-35, *"Peter answered and said unto Him, Though all men shall be offended because of thee, yet will I _____ be offended. (34) Jesus said unto him, Verily I say unto thee, That this night, before the cock _____, thou shalt deny me _____. (35) Peter said unto Him, Though I should _____ with thee, yet will I not deny thee. Likewise also said all the disciples."*

    He followed the crowd to the house of the high priest. By the time Peter arrived, Jesus had been taken inside to meet the high priest. We are not certain what time of the year it was, but we do know from the apostle John that it was cold; there was a fire built.

--John 18:18, *"And the servants and officers stood there, who had made a _____ of coals; for it was _____: and they warmed themselves: and Peter stood with them, and warmed himself."*

As Peter was warming himself by the fire a certain maid said in verse 56 of our text, *"...this man was also with Him."* Peter shot back in verse 57, *"...woman, I know Him not."* Minutes later, in verse 58, another person says, *"...thou art also of them..."* Peter replies, *"...man, I am not."*

Luke tells us in Luke 22:59, that *"...about the space of one hour..."* another spoke up and said, *"...of a truth this fellow also was with Him: for he is a Galilean."* Peter responds in verse 60, *"...man I know not what thou sayest..."* Peter is so agitated both Matthew and Mark let us know he began to curse and swear.

--Matthew 26:74, *"Then began he to _____ and to _____, saying I know not the man. And immediately the cock _____."*

--Mark 14:71, *"But he began to _____ and to _____, saying, I know not this man of whom ye speak."*

As the third denial left Peter's mouth, a rooster begins to crow. Peter realizes he has done exactly what Jesus told him he'd do. Peter has denied knowing Jesus three times before the rooster crowed. Peter was so depressed and remorseful we are told in Luke 22:62, *"...Peter went out, and wept bitterly."*

DISCUSSION: **Have you ever failed someone so badly that you cried over it?**
Are things better today? _____ Why? _____
_____
_____
_____

The gospels (Matthew, Mark, Luke, and John) are unanimous on one point. The rooster crowed at the exact moment of Peter's third denial. Suddenly it all became clear. This hidden memory of Peter pulled the rope that rang the bell of Peter's conscience. Peter remembered Jesus told him this was going to happen.

Luke's account of this story contains one detail the other writers do not include. Luke 22:61 says, *"...the Lord turned, and looked upon Peter..."* As addicts, we have hurt people badly and we are not able to look them in the eye. We are remorseful, repentant, and sorrowful. Eye contact causes our hearts to break. We know we are wrong! This is how Peter felt.

In this story of failure by the apostle Peter we must give Peter a little credit. At least he followed Jesus into the courtyard. The rest of the disciples would not even do this! The apostle John tells us in chapter eighteen there was one more present, but we are not sure of the circumstances!

Peter did not handle himself well, but at least he was there. His failure was terrible, but at least he cared enough to try and follow his Lord. This doesn't excuse his sin, but it does help us see the bigger picture more clearly.

We may try to achieve sobriety, yet fail. However, we must keep trying. We must remember God has more for us. God has a purpose for us. He had a purpose for Peter! Peter was forgiven and went on to do great things for God. He preached the first gospel sermon recorded in Acts chapter two. He taught many people about Jesus. Every time you find a list of apostles in the Bible, Peter is named first!

Jesus never criticized Peter and He never gave up on him! Jesus treats us the same way. He's not condemning us. He's offering us help.

Peter lost some things due to his failure. He lost his vanity, his pride, his self-confidence, his rash impulsiveness, and his unreliability. However, Peter gained much more. He gained humility, a new confidence in God, a tested courage, a new determination to serve Jesus, and a willingness to use his experience to help others!

The things Peter lost were things he really didn't need. The things he gained couldn't have come any other way. In the same way, God redeems our mistakes by taking away the things that brought us to our knees. He replaces those things with the qualities we were so desperately looking for, but could never see, because our addiction had us blinded.

DISCUSSION: What is one thing your addiction has kept you from doing?

_____

_____

_____

When God looks at us, He doesn't look and see only our failures. He sees beyond our faults to the loyalty underneath. He sees our pain, tears, and real desire to allow Him to help.

If Peter can fail, any of us can fail. We do. We fail miserably. But, if Peter can get back up, we can too!

My wife, children, and parents came to see me several times the last time I was in a rehabilitation facility. I always enjoyed their visits. My family is a part of my support system and I am thankful. I achieved sobriety for myself, my wife, my children, and my family. I told one of my daughters, "You have watched your father fall, now watch him get back up again." That is the attitude we must have. A dogged determination to find sobriety! If we seek it, we will find it. We can get back up again!

Where did this story of denial come from? It came from Peter. No one else was there to tell what happened. No one else was there to give details. This story had to come from Peter. Peter talked about it. I'm afraid we wouldn't do what Peter did. We try to hide our mistakes or blame others so no one finds out how human we are. If we are still trying to hide our addiction, we must stop. Everyone else already knows we're an addict. It's time we know it and admit it! If we think we are hiding our addiction from others, we are wrong. We are only hiding from ourselves!

Peter still speaks to us today. He says, "if you think you've fallen short, if you feel like you've hurt yourself and others, look at what happened to me. Don't stay down! Get back up! God loves you so much it doesn't matter what you've done. If God will forgive me, He will forgive anybody!"

DISCUSSION: Do you feel you've done things that are so bad God won't forgive you? _____

DISCUSSION: What does the scripture below say about ALL sin being forgiven?
_____
_____
_____
_____

--1 John 1:7-10, *"But if we walk in the light, as He is in the light, we have fellowship one with another, and the blood of Jesus Christ His Son cleanseth us from all _____. (8) If we say that we have no sin, we _____ ourselves, and the truth is not in us. (9) If we _____ our sins, He is faithful and just to forgive us our sins, and to cleanse us from all _____. (10) If we say that we have not sinned, we make Him a _____, and His word is not in us."*

There is hope for all of us. There is hope for the best of us, the worst of us, and the rest of us. If you, or someone you care about, is in active addiction, God can help. He can make us whole again. If we've failed, He can make us useful again. If we've lost the will to go on, He can help us find it.

ABOUT THE AUTHOR

Jonathan "Jon" Fears was born and raised in Northeast Arkansas. He married his wife, Lisa, on May 14, 1994. They have been married for twenty-nine years. They have four wonderful children: Sam, Gracie, Abigail, and Olivia.

Jon graduated from Arkansas Tech University, in Russellville, Arkansas, in May of 1995, with a Bachelor of Arts in Psychology degree.

Jon went on to earn a Master of Arts in Christian Counseling Psychology degree, in May of 2000, from Southwest Bible College & Seminary, in Humble, Texas.

Finally, Jon graduated with a Doctor of Arts in Ministry degree, in May of 2005, from Southwest Bible College & Seminary, in Humble, Texas.

Jon is a former addict who has struggled with addiction through the years. At times, his addiction has caused him to be arrested, convicted, and incarcerated. Jon has also spent many months in rehabilitation facilities as a result of his addictions.

Jon also happens to have a thorough knowledge of God's Word. He is a fourth-generation minister and has preached at many congregations throughout Northeast Arkansas and Southeast Missouri.

Jon knows what it's like to struggle with addiction. He chooses to use his life experiences to help families who also struggle with addiction.

Jon hopes to be contacted by those who are seeking help for themselves, or for someone they love! His email is fearsjon8@gmail.com.

Made in the USA
Middletown, DE
24 December 2024